MY ANCESTOR WAS A FREEMASON

Pat Lewis

Society of Genealogists

Published by

Society of Genealogists
14 Charterhouse Buildings
Goswell Road
London EC1M 7BA

Registered Charity No. 233701

© Pat Lewis 1999

ISBN 1 85951 405 7

British Library Cataloguing in Publication Data

A CIP Catalogue record for this book is available from the British Library

Pat Lewis is Vice-President of the Essex Society for Family History and President of the Fordham Local History Society, Essex. She has written three books about Fordham: *A big round hand*, on eduction; *This barren land*, concerning the Countess of Huntingdon's Connexion; and *A guide to All Saints Church*.

CONTENTS

Basic information
Introduction	1
A brief history of Freemasonry	2
What is a Freemason?	2
Masonic officers	3
The United Grand Lodge	3
Freemasons' Hall	4
Genealogical information and charges	4

Masonic publications
The Constitutions	5
Handbooks	5
Year Books	5
Data Protection Act 1984	6

Avenues of research
Quarter Sessions records	7
Craft Lodges (Private Lodges)	8
Other orders	12
Quatuor Coronati Lodge No. 2076	12
Provincial Grand Lodges	12
Other Grand Lodges under the British Constitution	13

Women Freemasons
The Order of Women Freemasons	14
The Honourable Fraternity of Ancient Freemasons	14

Military Lodges, prisoners of war and war memorials
Military Lodges	16
Prisoners of war	17
War memorials	18

Further information
Funerals and monumental inscriptions	19
Libraries, museums and record offices	20
Newspapers and illustrations	20
The Internet	21

Symbols and working tools	22
Regalia	
The apron	23
Collars, sashes and gauntlets	24
Hats	24
Jewels and medals	24
A word of warning	26
Certificates	
Lodge and Grand Lodge certificates	29
Other certificates	29
Artefacts	
China	32
Glass	32
Plate	33
Masonic charities	
The Grand Charity	34
The Royal Masonic Institution for Girls	34
The Royal Masonic Institution for Boys	34
The Masonic Trust for Boys and Girls	35
The Royal Masonic Benevolent Institution	35
The Royal Masonic Hospital and The New Samaritan Fund	36
Basic starting points	37
General comment	38
Select bibliography	40
Useful addresses	41
Index	45

PLATES

I	Craft Lodge officers' jewels	9
II	Master Mason's apron post-1815 and a reigning Worshipful Master	10
III	The square and compasses	22
IV	Master Mason's apron pre-1815	23
V	Masonic jewels	25
VI	A Freemason (Royal Arch, nineteenth century) and a non-Freemason (Royal Antediluvian Order of Buffaloes, nineteenth century)	27
VII	Friendly Society aprons using Masonic symbolism	28
VIII	A United Grand Lodge certificate in English and Latin	30
IX	Masonic artefacts	32

Plates II and VI: line drawings are by John Kay of the Millrind Press, Fordham, Essex CO6 3NQ, taken from photographs in the possession of the author.

Plates I, III, IV, V, VII, VIII and IX: illustrations are from material provided by the Board of General Purposes of the United Grand Lodge of England.

ACKNOWLEDGEMENTS

Unless otherwise stated the illustrations are from the collections of The United Grand Lodge of England. I am grateful to the Board of General Purposes of The United Grand Lodge of England for permission to reproduce the illustrations and to use material from their pamphlets. I would also like to thank the library of The United Grand Lodge for their assistance while producing this booklet.

To the following my thanks for their computer expertise, help, encouragement and patience: Mike Barker, Donald Grimes, Helen and Mike Hipkin, Clayton Lewis and Peter Neivens, OBE, QPM.

The drawing of a man wearing the regalia of a member of the Royal Antediluvian Order of Buffaloes (Plate VI) is based upon a photograph submitted by Mrs Anne L Jacques of Leeds to *Family Tree Magazine* and published in June 1994 (page 18).

BASIC INFORMATION

Introduction

This booklet is for the family historian who is trying to find information about ancestors who could have been Freemasons, and possibly portraits or photographs of them. I am not a Freemason, and have found that to research Masonic ancestors a knowledge of ritual is unnecessary; therefore it has no part in this booklet.

You may have been told that some member of your family was a Freemason or a pupil, boy or girl, at a Masonic school; you may know where or when this person lived, or whether he or she received Masonic charity. Artefacts such as china, glass, certificates, aprons, jewels and other regalia are frequently inherited without any information regarding their origin. Is it possible to confirm whether they are Masonic or from some other organisation? In every case the style decoration and colour can tell you much about your forbears' Masonic career. An introduction to this complicated subject is necessary, and an excellent one is the *Freemasons' guide and compendium* by B E Jones (1956). If it is possible, visit the museum at Freemasons' Hall in London, to study their magnificent collections and seek their advice.

The information in this booklet is limited to England and Wales, which are under the jurisdiction of The United Grand Lodge. It must be understood that the number of men who have been Freemasons within the English Constitution could run into millions, and as every Freemason must first be a member of a Craft Lodge, the search has to begin with Craft Freemasonry. There are many other orders in Freemasonry, and these will be dealt with very briefly. Women Freemasons are discussed separately. A considerable amount of information can be found in record offices, libraries and bookshops, and it would be wise to try these sources first.

Until the 1930s, in Europe Freemasons took part freely in public life. They held processions in towns, and laid foundation stones without detrimental comment. However, in Germany, with the rise of the Nazis in the 1930s, Freemasons and Jews were vilified and the Freemasons went to ground until the end of the Second World War. During this time one method of recognition used in Europe by Freemasons was a very small forget-me-not badge which was worn under the lapel. In England the fear of invasion in 1940 persuaded Freemasons to withdraw from public scrutiny, and this reticence lingered on until the early 1980s when a policy of 'openness' was decided upon. In an address, at Grand Lodge in 1994, The Grand Master, HRH The Duke of Kent, KG said, 'One way to promote greater understanding is to persevere in our efforts at every level to demonstrate how much about Freemasonry can be shared with people who are not Masons, particularly our families'. It is to be hoped that this statement will lead to the opening of many avenues of research into Masonic ancestry.

A brief history of Freemasonry

The origins of Freemasonry are obscure; some scholars place and argue over origins which date back to ancient Egypt but this remains conjecture. Speculative Masonry (non-operative) as opposed to Operative Masonry (actual workers) stems from the middle of the seventeenth century at about the time that the Royal Society was founded for the organised research into the hidden mysteries of nature and science. It would appear that the terminology used by the Masons' Guilds was employed to express a view of morality.

In 1813, The United Grand Lodge of Antient, Free and Accepted Masons of England was formed from the Premier Grand Lodge of 1717 and the Atholl Grand Lodge of 1753. It is known today as The United Grand Lodge. The Freemasons' view of charity, which includes widows and orphans, helped to spread a voluntary ideal, and the manner in which the Master of a Lodge was selected for that office, regardless of social status, implanted in English thinking a new appreciation of the man rather than the office. For a detailed history of Freemasonry, see *World Freemasonry* by J Hamill and R A Gilbert (1991), the *Freemasons' guide and compendium* by B E Jones (1956), and *Freemasonry* by W K McNulty (1991).

What is a Freemason?

Popular myth suggests that a Freemason was a white Anglican Conservative from the middle class or above; but as stated in the third edition of the *Spirit of Masonry* by W Hutchinson, published in 1802, 'Pride not yourselves on your birth, or your honours or your riches. I reduce all conditions to a pleasing and rational equality'. Thus it can be seen that Freemasons came from a very wide section of society.

The following requirements are stated in *The Constitutions* of The United Grand Lodge and various pamphlets including *Freemasonry and religion* and *What is Freemasonry?* All of these can be seen at Freemasons' Hall or are obtainable from the bookshop.

A Freemason must be at least 21 years old, except in Apollo University Lodge, No. 357 (Oxford) and Isaac Newton University Lodge, No. 859 (Cambridge), when acceptance is possible at 18 years of age.

He can be of any social class which means that an artisan could be the Master of a Lodge who accepted a member of the upper classes into the Lodge, or vice versa.

He can follow any occupation.

He can be of any race or colour.

He can be of any political persuasion.

He can be of any religion or denomination, but must profess a belief in a Supreme Being.

He must declare any criminal connection in his application for membership.

Masonic officers

The following information can help you with your research.

A Grand Officer is appointed by The Grand Master from any Lodge in England or Wales.

London Grand Rank Officers are appointed from London Lodges by The Grand Master.

Provincial Grand Lodge officers are appointed by The Provincial Grand Master of the Province to which they belong.

Worshipful Master is the highest office appointed by a Craft Lodge.

Craft Lodge officers are appointed by the Worshipful Master of the Lodge.

The complex situation regarding ranks is further explained in *The Constitutions* by The United Grand Lodge.

The United Grand Lodge

The United Grand Lodge of Antient, Free and Accepted Masons of England, which includes Wales, is the governing body of Freemasons and has superintending authority of altering, repealing and enacting laws and regulations for the Craft and also has power to investigate and regulate matters pertaining to the craft, particularly regarding Lodges or individual brothers. The head of The United Grand Lodge is The Most Worshipful The Grand Master. For the history read the *Freemasons' guide and compendium* by B E Jones (1956); for constitutions and regulations *The Constitutions* and for further information the current *Masonic Year Book*, all of which are obtainable from Letchworth's bookshop at Freemasons' Hall, London.

Freemasons' Hall

The present Freemasons' Hall is situated in Great Queen Street, London WC2B 5AZ, telephone 0171 831 9811, and was built as a Masonic Peace Memorial after the 1914-18 war. At Freemasons' Hall there is a permanent exhibition of the history of English Freemasonry and a Masonic museum, library and First World War memorial, all of which are open to everyone. If you wish to research in the library, the procedure for record offices applies and it is wise to contact the librarian regarding an appointment and to explain your research project. Owing to the fragile nature of many membership books they are not available for individual study and are only handled by the staff.

Freemasons' Hall is open to the public on weekdays, free of charge, from 10.00 to 17.00, Saturdays 10.00 to 13.00 but not on Sundays or public holidays (including the Saturdays preceding public holidays). In normal circumstances conducted tours of Freemasons' Hall and The Grand Temple, from the museum, are available hourly from 11.00 to 16.00. Arrangements can be made for organised conducted tours for groups of people on Saturday mornings, by application to the Grand Secretary. For a guide to Freemasons' Hall and its contents read *Freemasons' Hall* by J Stubbs and T O Haunch (1983). Letchworth's bookshop is in the foyer where Masonic books, videos, audio tapes and souvenirs can be purchased by anyone, and the availability of these items can be checked by ordering a catalogue.

Genealogical information and charges

For details of the scope of this information write to the assistant librarian, and for other services which they may offer see various sections in this booklet. There are set search fees for members and non-members, but if the Lodge name and number are known there is no charge. At the present time these charges are under review and a sliding scale may be introduced. Write to the assistant librarian at Freemasons' Hall for details and application form.

MASONIC PUBLICATIONS

The Constitutions

This is The United Grand Lodge's rule book which contains the full 'basic principles' and a statement on the aims and relationships of the craft. Family historians will find excellent descriptions and illustrations of jewels and regalia. It can be bought from Freemasons' Hall, London, or try your county library.

Handbooks

Handbooks have been published annually by Provincial Grand Lodges at various dates depending on the Province. In Essex, for example, these commenced in 1886. They contain details of Craft Lodges and other Masonic orders, for example Mark Masonry or Royal Ark Mariners in the county, the registered number of the Lodges, dates when formed, venue and a list of officers and secretaries' addresses. These handbooks, some of which have been deposited in record offices and libraries, can include historic Masonic events of interest in the county, and some of these events may have been reported in local or national newspapers. They can also be seen at Freemasons' Hall, Provincial Grand Lodges or at local Lodges.

Year Books

From 1790 a Calendar was published annually containing very varied information and since 1908 a Masonic Year Book has been published annually by The United Grand Lodge of England and contains numerical and alphabetical lists of Craft Lodges and other orders, with the dates when they were formed. It records where and when Lodges meet, both at home and abroad, together with details of The United Grand Lodge and its officers, Provincial Grand Lodges, District Grand Lodges, Commonwealth and Foreign Grand Lodges and their secretaries. There are also details of various charities and historic Masonic events. Some Year Books have been deposited in record offices and libraries or can be seen at Freemasons' Hall in London, where the current edition can be purchased in the bookshop. A *Masonic Year Book historical supplement* (1969), was published under the authority of The United Grand Lodge. This gives extensive nominal lists of office holders of Grand Rank, 1717 to 1968, appointed by the Grand Master. Another supplement was published covering the period 1969 to 1976. Both of these can be seen in the library at United Grand Lodge with the first mentioned in the library of the Society of Genealogists. These supplements can be useful for anyone whose ancestor held such an office. The date of appointment is given and in most cases the date of his death. From these two events it is possible that United Grand Lodge could find more information regarding his Lodge and where he lived.

Data Protection Act 1984

The use of computers in Masonic Lodge administration and for historical records is becoming widespread. If secretaries or treasurers use a computer they also have, under *The Constitutions*, rules 144 and 153, to keep the records in book form. The Data Protection Act applies to people who keep personal details about living persons on a computer which is intended to be processed in some form. The United Grand Lodge is sensitive to this issue and does not welcome queries regarding living persons; however, names do appear in handbooks and Year Books both before and after 1984. As in all societies, including family history societies, members have to be asked whether they object to their name being included on a computer database. If they object their name must be immediately taken off and the information has to be held and dealt within a paper file, that is, manually. For more information about this Act read *Guidelines: general legal matters*, leaflet from The Federation of Family History Societies (1993), or *The Data Protection Act and genealogists*, leaflet No. 18 from the Society of Genealogists (revised edn. 1997). A word of warning, the new Data Protection Act, 1998, which comes into effect early 1999, alters some legal requirements.

AVENUES OF RESEARCH

It is advisable to begin your research with the Quarter Sessions records which should have been deposited in the record office of the county in which your ancestor's Lodge met. This is likely to be the county in which he lived or worked. An exception, for example, is a man who lived in south Essex, worked in London and belonged to a Lodge in Suffolk. His name appears in the 1967 Quarter Sessions records in the Suffolk Record Office. He had strong family connections with Suffolk where he had lived and had been educated, and permission was obtained for him to join a Lodge a considerable distance from where he lived or worked. This is a case where elderly relatives can provide the vital clue.

Quarter Sessions records

In the aftermath of the French Revolution, in the late eighteenth century, there was considerable suspicion of societies and organisations which had meetings where members were sworn in and oaths were taken. This led to the Seditious Societies Act, Geo.III 39 c.79, 1799, under which all societies where members were required to take any oath not authorised by law were deemed to be unlawful combinations. Regular Lodges of Freemasons whose meetings were mainly directed towards charitable purposes were not proscribed by the Act, providing that members' names were certified annually to the Clerk of the Peace, and Quarter Sessions were empowered to close any Lodge if a complaint was upheld. Freemasonry, then, was never considered to be a dangerous 'secret society', and family historians can make enquiries with confidence.

Quarter Sessions records provide:

(a) A register of Lodges of Freemasons whose annual certificates of members' names had been received at Quarter Sessions. This register gives number, name, place and time of meeting of each Lodge.

(b) Annual certificates from Lodges giving number, name, place and time of meeting of each Lodge, with names of members and their abode and occupation. These certificates do not give a date of birth or age, but these are given in Lodge membership books. Many of these certificates were signed personally by the Master and Secretary of the Lodge. If Lodge records are unobtainable, a surviving certificate or certificates in your family papers may be the only method of determining whether your ancestor held these offices in his Lodge. By looking at these certificates it is possible to find whether a Freemason changed his address or occupation; they can be particularly useful in tracing movement before civil registration began in 1837. If Lodge records are not available, certificates also make it possible to calculate the length of time taken for a man to become the Master of his Lodge.

If you know where your ancestor lived but not to which Lodge he belonged, it is advisable to contact the Provincial Grand Lodge of the county, to find the numbers and venues of the Lodges in existence in that county at the time in which you are interested. As it was usual for a man to join a Lodge near to where he lived or worked, you can draw a circle on a map, consider the distance and difficulties of travel at the time chosen, and search the Quarter Sessions records for that area.

In these records your ancestors' companions are shown, not only social companions but possibly extended family connections, as many men attended a Lodge with relatives from both male and female lines. They can also be a source of information regarding names you have come across but have been unable to trace, which can then be followed in directories, parish registers etc.

Quarter Sessions records have been deposited in county record offices and the years relevant to the study of Freemasonry are 1799 to 1967 when, under the Criminal Law Act 1967, Eliz.II 15-16 Pt.1 c.58 p.1214, registers of lodges and annual certificates were no longer necessary. Unfortunately, in some counties the coverage is patchy. The returns were sent to the Clerk of the Peace and some may still be languishing in county council archives. Advice in this booklet is largely restricted to information referring to people who are no longer living, but the Quarter Sessions records are public records and open to public scrutiny. If these records do not supply the information you require, the next step is to make enquiries from various Lodges.

For further information regarding these records see *Quarter Sessions records for family historians* (4th edn.) compiled by J S W Gibson, which gives holdings available in various record offices.

Craft Lodges (Private Lodges)

In attempting to obtain more details concerning an ancestor who was a Freemason the search has to begin here, as a Craft Lodge is the first Lodge into which every Freemason must be initiated. By a system of degrees or stages he may advance to

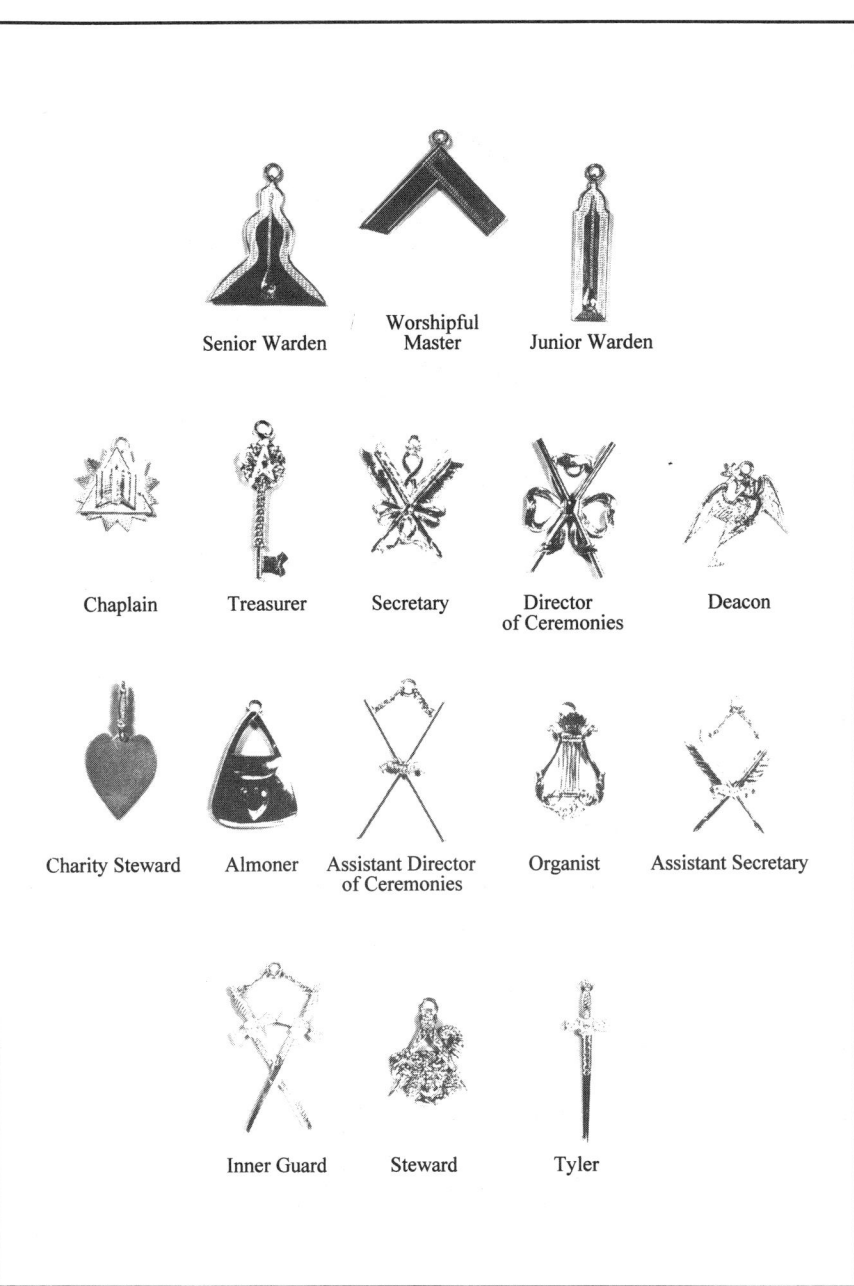

Plate I – Craft Lodge officers' jewels

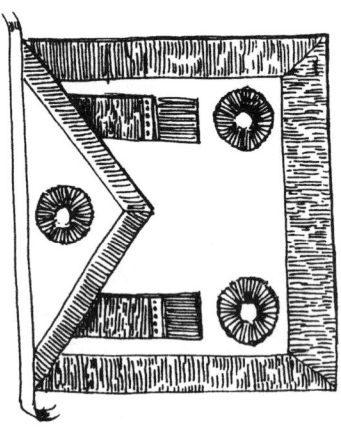

Master Mason's apron post-1815

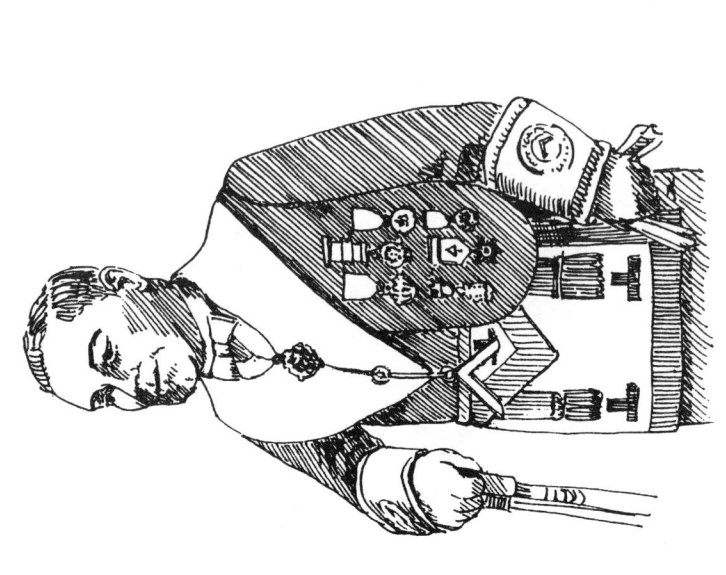

A reigning Worshipful Master

Plate II

become a Master Mason and when he has served in various offices in his Lodge (note that each office has its own jewel) he may be elected to the highest office of a Craft Lodge, that of the Worshipful Master. It is usual to hold this office for one year and it can only be held for a maximum of two years in succession. There are other offices in which he may serve, and for details of all offices in a Lodge see *The Constitutions* by The United Grand Lodge. (Plates I and II.)

Every Lodge which is under the jurisdiction of The United Grand Lodge has a registered number. Some Lodges are no longer in existence and their Lodge number would not have been reissued. If a Lodge was formed before 1863 the number will have been changed, but since that date Lodge numbers have not been altered. For detailed information regarding the number of the Lodge you are researching, if it was registered before 1863 or is one which you are unable to trace, write to the librarian at Freemasons' Hall.

In most Lodges there is on display a dated list of all their Worshipful Masters since the Lodge was formed, and there may also be photographs or portraits of some of them. Many Lodges have produced Lodge histories and these can be a rich source for family historians of photographs and lists of names. Try the Lodge or the Provincial Grand Lodge concerned.

Finding Lodge records is not easy, but perseverence can pay dividends. A bonus for family historians in this 'time of openness' is that some Lodges have deposited their records in county record offices. It is advisable that your research should begin at the appropriate county record office regarding any deposits of Lodge records or Quarter Sessions records.

Masonic Year Books have details of every Craft Lodge in existence at the time of publication, both alphabetically and numerically, together with their meeting places. Provincial Grand Lodge handbooks give further details and addresses to contact and it is often possible to find the addresses and telephone numbers of Masonic halls in the telephone directory. If Lodges have kept their membership books they should be able to help you. A Lodge membership book I have seen has the following heading: members' names, profession, residence, age, date of admission, and remarks (which can include when the member died or resigned, if he came from another Lodge or if he moved to another Lodge). This information could be invaluable when trying to trace a member's movements. If seeking information regarding Lodges no longer in existence or Lodges which were working during the period of your research, consult Quarter Sessions records or contact the appropriate Provincial Grand Lodge or the librarian at Freemasons' Hall.

When making enquiries it is best to state why you want the information and your involvement with the person named. When you contact Lodge officials remember that they, like those in family history societies, are volunteers, and their time for research may be restricted as the number of meetings held annually by individual Lodges varies considerably. Always remember to enclose an s.a.e. whenever you write for information.

This is an intricate subject and there are two other publications which offer more information. For general information there is the *Freemasons' guide and compendium* by B E Jones (1956), and, regarding Lodge numbers and names, *Serendipity* by Harry Mendoza (1995).

Other Orders

There are many other orders in Freemasonry such as Mark Masonry and Royal Ark Mariners, and these are listed in Provincial Grand Lodge handbooks, but do remember that every Freemason has first to join a Craft Lodge.

Quatuor Coronati Lodge No. 2076

This Lodge was established for the study of Masonic history and meets at Freemasons' Hall, London. Papers which are read and discussed at these meetings are subsequently published in *Ars Quatuor Coronatorum* – the transactions of the Lodge – and these, together with a list of the principal contents from 1886, can be researched in the library at Freemasons' Hall, where offprints and photocopies may be available for a small charge. These transactions contain background information regarding Masonic ancestors who were either emigrants or immigrants, and many names are often included. References, given under various subjects (for example Military Lodges), can assist your research. These volumes may be available at Provincial Grand Lodges, and since Volume 90 in 1977, they have been published with an International Standard Book Number and should therefore be obtainable through county libraries.

Provincial Grand Lodges

Provincial Grand Lodges have jurisdiction over all Lodges in their Province or District. *The Masonic Year Book* from The United Grand Lodge which has details of its officers, Provinces, names and numbers of Lodges, both alphabetically and numerically, covers the whole country, and includes addresses. Each Provincial Lodge issues its own handbook with similar information regarding its own Province, usually with telephone numbers of Lodge secretaries. Telephone numbers of Masonic halls can also be found, in most cases, in the appropriate telephone directory. There are forty-seven Provincial Grand Lodges in England and Wales, the largest being West Lancashire with over five hundred Lodges.

In many Provincial Grand Lodges, archivists are now at work sorting archival material and collecting copies of Lodge histories, pamphlets, etc. If the voluntary manpower is available they may answer varied questions including genealogical queries, but they may not have the same research facilities available to them as the library at Freemasons' Hall. The number of Lodges in a Province, together with the names, numbers and venues at any given date, can easily be ascertained by a letter or telephone call to the Provincial Grand Lodge concerned. This information can be valuable to narrow your search if you know where your ancestor lived or worked, but not to which Lodge he belonged, especially if the Lodge to which he could have belonged is no longer in existence.

Other Grand Lodges under the British Constitution

These Grand Lodges cover the rest of the world and details appear in the *Masonic Year Book* from The United Grand Lodge. Included are details of the Grand Lodge of Ireland and the Grand Lodge of Scotland, together with Commonwealth and Foreign Grand Lodges.

WOMEN FREEMASONS

If you saw a portrait of a woman in Masonic regalia would you assume that she was wearing her husband's regalia? If this would be your reaction, further research might provide a different explanation. There is evidence of women members of a Masons' Company in 1663 and 1713/14, but women were expressly excluded from Freemasons' Lodges in the first edition of *The Constitutions* produced in 1723 and in every subsequent edition since then. However, there are women Freemasons at the present time in London, the Provinces, Wales, Scotland, Northern Ireland and Eire, the Channel Islands, Australia, Canada and elsewhere overseas. There are now two groups of Women Freemasons in England, both of which admit women only and practise exactly the same rituals and degree ceremonies, wear the same regalia and use the same titles as their male counterparts.

The Order of Women Freemasons

1902 Co-Masonry, a mixed Lodge of men and women, was introduced into England and known as the Lodge of Human Duty.

1908 A group of men and women from the Lodge of Human Duty set up the Honourable Fraternity of Antient Masonry which, since 1935, has been known as the Order of Women Freemasons, admitting women only. Their headquarters are in London. This is the larger of the two orders and now has approximately 347 Lodges over the country and many abroad. The address of The Order of Women Freemasons is 27 Pembridge Gardens, London W2 4EF, telephone 0171 229 2368.

The Honourable Fraternity of Ancient Freemasons

1913 A group seceded from The Honourable Fraternity of Antient Masonry and formed the Honourable Fraternity of Ancient Freemasons whose headquarters are also in London. They have forty-nine Lodges in this country and one in Gibraltar. They have privately published *The Honourable Fraternity of Ancient Freemasons, 1913-1988* by D S Granatt, which is an excellent history full of illustrations.

Their address is: The Honourable Fraternity of Ancient Freemasons, The Grand Temple, 68 Great Cumberland Place, London W1H 7FD, telephone 0171 723 9526.

An illustrated book, *Women in the Craft - the story of feminine Freemasonry* by F W Seal-Coon and R A Gilbert is about to be published (1998) by Quatuor Coronati Lodge. For details enquire at the library at Freemasons' Hall.

MILITARY LODGES, PRISONERS OF WAR AND WAR MEMORIALS

The spread of Craft Masonry abroad was largely due to Military Lodges. In the 1730s Military Lodges were issued with travelling warrants which allowed them to hold a meeting wherever the regiment was stationed, and most regiments in the British Army had at least one Lodge. In 1732 the Grand Lodge of Ireland issued the first warrant to the First Battalion of the Royal Scots Regiment; in 1747, the Grand Lodge of Scotland warranted the Duke of Norfolk's 12th Foot (later the Suffolk Regiment). Following this the United Grand Lodge warranted many Military Lodges including the Militia and Fencible Cavalry Regiments, Naval and other Field Lodges all over the world, and this extended in time to include airmen.

Military Lodges

In 'The Master Mason at arms by Frederic Smythe, published in *Ars Quatuor Coronatorum* in 1990, he explained the situation in detail and gave a warning that to research Freemasons who served between 1732 and 1949 in the British Army who were also members of Travelling Lodges is a difficult and complex task. Quarter Sessions records may be useful such as those of 1799 for Colchester in Essex (Essex Record Office Q/RSm 2/1) which show that the 11th Regiment of Foot, North Devon Lodge No. 313, had registered under the Seditious Societies Act of 1799, and list the names of members, their rank and position held, even including the regimental hairdresser. The Warwickshire Regiment of Militia Lodge also registered, with no venue mentioned, but the names of twenty soldiers are shown without their ranks. At the same time, under Angel Lodge No. 47 (now No. 51), several soldiers were registered who attended its Lodge meetings, for example a sergeant of artillery, members of the West Suffolk Militia and the Northumberland Militia. This is a good example of army personnel who were Freemasons attending a local Lodge, presumably while they were in transit. It is worth looking at Quarter Sessions records for garrison towns if you are researching a military or naval ancestor. These documents include the actual signature of the Worshipful Master and the Senior Warden or the secretary. In most cases Military Lodges were composed of both officers and other ranks.

The United Grand Lodge, The Grand Lodge of Ireland and The Scottish Grand Lodge may have records of some of the Travelling Lodges with names of members.

A very comprehensive list of Sea and Field Lodges in the seventeenth and eighteenth centuries can be found in *The history of Freemasonry*, vol.4, by R F Gould (revised 1952).

Prisoners of war

There were English prisoners in France during the Napoleonic Wars and it is known that individuals on parole attended French Lodges as guests. Details are scarce but in 'English prisoners of war in France' by A R Hewitt, a petition is discussed from the Département de la Moselle, dated June 1812, in which English prisoners of war are requesting a warrant for a Lodge. Twenty signatures are given together with their home Lodge name, number and venue – for example Bermondsey (London), Bristol and Guernsey. Freemasons in captivity in the First and Second World Wars, both in Europe and the Far East, are comprehensively discussed in 'Craftsmen in captivity' by A R Hewitt. This second paper is fully referenced and in some cases mention is made of names and notebooks having been deposited. These two papers can be found in *Ars Quatuor Coronatorum*, vol.77, (1964), and can be seen in the library at Freemasons' Hall.

In the museum at Freemasons' Hall there are displays of Masonic regalia made by prisoners of war from any materials available at the time, including coins, parts of a camp bed or a wrecked vehicle. There are items associated with the Boer War, German and Japanese prisoner of war camps, and the German occupation of the Channel Islands. A ritual book used in Germany bears the signature of some of those taking part, even though they risked death by so doing. In these recent wars there were no Lodges, as such, in prisoner of war camps but where brethren recognised each other they met together to practise whenever possible. In a few cases minutes were kept with names included and these have been deposited in museums such as the one at Freemasons' Hall.

In the museum at Freemasons' Hall, Masonic jewels can be seen which were made for sale by French prisoners from scraps which came to hand. Masonic French prisoners during the Seven Years War (1756-63) and the Napoleonic Wars were often shown hospitality by British Lodges. They also set up their own Lodges where they were imprisoned for example in Ashby-de-la-Zouch, Chesterfield, Derby, Thame and in prison hulks. There was even one in Malta. Some of these documents survive, giving signatures, ranks, regiments and various other details. Information regarding these can be found in *The Transactions of the Lodge of Research* No. 2429 (Leicester, 1924/25), in the library at Freemasons' Hall. It is possible that some of these prisoners did not return to France and have mysteriously appeared on your family tree! (Plate IX)

War Memorials

Freemasons' Hall in London was built as a World War One peace memorial; the memorial shrine, window and roll of honour can be seen in the first vestibule. The roll commemorates Freemasons who died in the First World War, and they are listed under their Lodge numbers. This roll of honour was published twice and may be found in libraries, the British Library or in an antiquarian bookshop. Nearby in the hall is another roll of honour which commemorates Freemasons who died in the Second World War and they are also listed under their Lodge numbers. Both of these rolls can be consulted by anyone. An illustrated description of the shrine is included in *Freemasons' Hall* by J Stubbs and T O Haunch (1983).

There may be memorials in some Masonic halls but this will need to be ascertained by personal enquiry.

For the Royal Masonic Institution for Boys Memorial Book, *see* page 35.

FURTHER INFORMATION

Funerals and monumental inscriptions

In the eighteenth and nineteenth centuries many Masonic funerals were conducted with full ceremonial and Freemasons, like Friendly Society members, were expected to attend a brother's funeral wearing regalia. In the *Freemasons' guide and compendium* by B E Jones (1956) there are details of how these ceremonies were conducted. Before the 1930s there were extensive reports in newspapers of Masonic funerals which included family details, civic and charitable interests, Masonic careers and the names of mourners. One report in 1926 even gives a photograph of the deceased and information regarding the whereabouts of a portrait in oils.

It is sometimes assumed that a skull and crossbones on a headstone indicate that the deceased was a Freemason, but this is not so; it was just a fashionable symbol of mortality. Masonic symbols can be seen on headstones in many burial places, the most common being the square and compasses, and there can be other signs including representations of masons' tools and the all seeing eye (*see* Symbols and working tools). A word of warning: some other societies used signs and symbols similar to those of the Freemasons such as The Royal Antediluvian Order of Buffaloes. Records of monumental inscriptions have been deposited with record offices, the Society of Genealogists and with family history societies. The Essex Society for Family History has published a booklet *Finding Essex monumental inscriptions* compiled by C Lewis, which covers all the parishes in their area and indicates whether the inscriptions are recorded or not and where they have been deposited. It is worth making enquiries of local family history societies to find whether they have produced a similar list.

Libraries, museums and record offices

The library at Freemasons' Hall is undoubtedly the best Masonic library and is open to all. They have a large collection of published and unpublished works, prints, engravings, pictures, charts, drawings, photographs of people or Masonic occasions and many other documents. Public libraries may contain newspapers and Lodge histories and they can obtain most books mentioned in this booklet and in some circumstances, with rare books, can obtain photocopies. If the information required still eludes you, write to the library at Freemasons' Hall which is a reference library only, and they may supply photocopies. If you wish to buy any of the books mentioned, your library will be able to inform you if the book is still in print.

The museum at Freemasons' Hall is open to all and has the most comprehensive collection of Masonic material that can be seen anywhere. There is a large collection of illustrations of events, photographs and a picture gallery. For a description, see *Freemasons' Hall* by J Stubbs and T O Haunch (1983) which also contains details of the library. For both the museum and the library ring or write to Freemasons' Hall, Great Queen Street, London WC2B 5AZ, telephone 0171 831 9811.

County record offices hold the returns to Quarter Sessions, though the coverage may be patchy. They may have some Lodge histories, Masonic year books or handbooks and runs of newspapers. Masonic Lodges have begun to deposit their records with record offices and the Essex and Suffolk Record Offices are among the first to receive such deposits. *Record offices: how to find them* (7th edn.) compiled by J S W Gibson, will simplify your quest.

Newspapers and illustrations

Newspapers are a rich source for illustrations of events and photographs of ancestors. Similar to Friendly Societies and Trade Unions, Freemasons took part in processions to various events wearing regalia, with banners flying, bands playing, and relevant reports may often be found in newspapers. On special occasions Freemasons left their meeting place, frequently a public house, and walked in Masonic order to the church and then returned. You may also find reports of meetings of Provincial Grand Lodges, theatre visits, the laying of foundation stones, funerals, etc., and from these reports venues and names may be found. For example, in the late eighteenth century, the *Ipswich Journal* reported details of theatre performances in Colchester, where named Freemasons formed a Lodge on the stage, and on another occasion a Masonic ode was sung. In both these reports some names were given and similar reports can be found in newspapers in other parts of the country.

Many Freemasons' magazines have been produced, including *The Masonic Mirror, The Freemasons' Quarterly Review, Freemasons Journal* and *Freemasonry Today*. They cover the whole country and include many names together with reports of meetings. Copies of these can be seen at the library at Freemasons' Hall. Some handbooks and Year Books have a section on Masonic events of interest, with dates, which point to events which could have appeared in newspapers and magazines, once again providing names and possibly illustrations.

For information regarding newspapers read *Local newspapers 1750-1920: A select location list* compiled by J S W Gibson (1987). The British Library Newspaper Library, is at Colindale Avenue, London NW9 5HE, and there is a working catalogue of the library in the reading room. There is also a published version of this catalogue, consisting of eight volumes containing entries as they stood at the end of 1971, and a copy of this can be seen at the Society of Genealogists.

The Internet

The Internet is a network which joins together a large number of computer networks. If you are looking for Masonic information there are numerous foreign and United Kingdom Websites. In 1997 The United Grand Lodge launched an Internet home page, and websites have been set up for the Provinces of Jersey, Somerset, Dorset, Berkshire and East Lancashire; these are linked to the The United Grand Lodge Home Page. All contain general information and more websites are set to follow.

The United Grand Lodge http://www.grand-lodge.org.

London Freemasonry http://www.london-lodges.org

SYMBOLS AND WORKING TOOLS

Friendly Societies and some Trade Unions (for example The Ancient Order of Foresters, The Independent Order of Odd Fellows, The Royal Antediluvian Order of Buffaloes and The United Society of Brushmakers) borrowed from Freemasonry an organisational pattern and the use of symbols, decorated costume and regalia

Freemasonry uses much symbolism, the square and compasses being the most common. Some of the symbols, which have also been used by various associations, are the beehive, the all seeing eye and faith, hope and charity. If the material you have does not expressly mention to which association it belongs, further research will be needed; a symbol of itself does not necessarily indicate to which association your ancestor belonged. The library at United Grand Lodge may be able to help, and Masonic symbolism is discussed in the *Freemasons' guide and compendium* by   B E Jones (1956). (Plate III.)

Plate III – The Square and Compasses.

REGALIA

Regalia is the clothing, insignia and jewels (medals) worn by a Freemason, and before the introduction of standard patterns in 1815 many different designs were used. You may have inherited items of regalia and not realised that it is possible to discover much about your ancestor from them. (Plate II.)

The apron

Masonic aprons can denote the order in Freemasonry and the position held in that order by the owner. In early times, Operative Masons in trade Guilds were recognisable by their long, thick leather aprons with a raised flap, and the first English Speculative Masons wore aprons usually made of white lambskin, some of which were decorated according to the wishes of the owner. They could be painted, embroidered or printed with many kinds of symbols and emblems and allegorical figures.

Plate IV – Master Mason's apron pre-1815.

The standard patterns insisted upon in 1815 were very similar to those in use today. As a guide, a pale blue apron denotes a member of a Craft Lodge, a dark blue apron a member of a Provincial Lodge and there are other colours which show membership of various other orders. The first apron which a man owns and keeps in his possession is the Master Mason's Apron which is lambskin trimmed with watered sky-blue silk edges, and decorated with three sky-blue rosettes and two silver tassels. If a man becomes the reigning Worshipful Master of his Lodge the rosettes are changed to squares and a large jewel in the form of a square hangs from his collar and the name of his Lodge may be seen on his gauntlets. It is a reasonable proposition that a photograph of your ancestor in Masonic regalia would have been taken when he held the office of Worshipful Master. (Plates II and IV.)

Collars, sashes and gauntlets

For hundreds of years in public life collars have been worn as a distinguishing mark of office. In Freemasonry collars denote that an office is held in a Lodge, and appended to the collar is the jewel of that office. A sash is not worn by Craft Masons but can be worn in other orders. In the eighteenth century plain white gauntleted gloves were worn, but these became so elaborately ornamented that ease of movement was difficult, and the gauntlets were then detached. Before 1883 they were worn from personal choice but now *The Constitutions* of The United Grand Lodge states that certain officers should, or in some cases may, wear gauntlets, and these usually have the name of the Province or the name of the Lodge embroidered on them. This is a point to remember when trying to identify photographs.

Hats

In the eighteenth century the Master of a Lodge wore a hat. Nowadays, in some Bristol Lodges the Master wears a cocked hat, and in Pilgrim Lodge, No. 238, London, a German-speaking Lodge, the members wear top hats.

Jewels and medals

In all orders of Freemasonry, jewels (medals) denoting rank, office, presentation or commemoration of notable events are worn with Masonic regalia. These jewels, of great beauty, are now collected and there are thousands of different designs in existence. The museum at Freemasons' Hall has a magnificent collection with a register available for reference, and this lists all Lodges under their jurisdiction and the jewels associated with them which are held in the reserve collection. (Plate V.)

Plate V – Masonic Jewels.

In order to identify a photograph of anyone wearing regalia, or any regalia in your possession, *The Constitutions* of The United Grand Lodge and *Freemasons' Hall* by J Stubbs and T O Haunch (1983) are useful as they contain illustrations of many types of regalia. After enquiries at a local Craft Lodge or a Provincial Grand Lodge, write to, or visit, the museum at Freemasons' Hall where there is a large collection of regalia. When making a postal enquiry to any of the above, enclose a photograph and they will do their best to assist you. Regarding people, it is unlikely that without the name or number of the Lodge, Freemason's Hall will be able to identify an individual, but only the position held and possibly the Province. You can then make enquiries to the Province or Lodge in question and you may find out who is shown in the photograph. A book, *The medals of the Masonic fraternity described and illustrated* by W T R Marvin, is due to be reprinted (1998) by Quatuor Coronati Lodge. For details enquire at the library at Freemasons' Hall.

A word of warning!

Friendly Societies and Trade Unions also wore regalia very similar to that of the Freemasons, for example sashes, gauntlets and aprons. It is advisable to make careful enquiries to ensure whether the regalia or material in your possession is Masonic or otherwise. The museum at Freemasons' Hall will be able to help, and in the case of The Royal Antediluvian Order of Buffaloes, whose regalia is remarkably similar to that of the Freemasons, the catalogues of Toye, Kenning and Spencer Ltd., regalia specialists of 19-21, Great Queen Street, London WC2B 5BE, can be very helpful. (Plates VI and VII.)

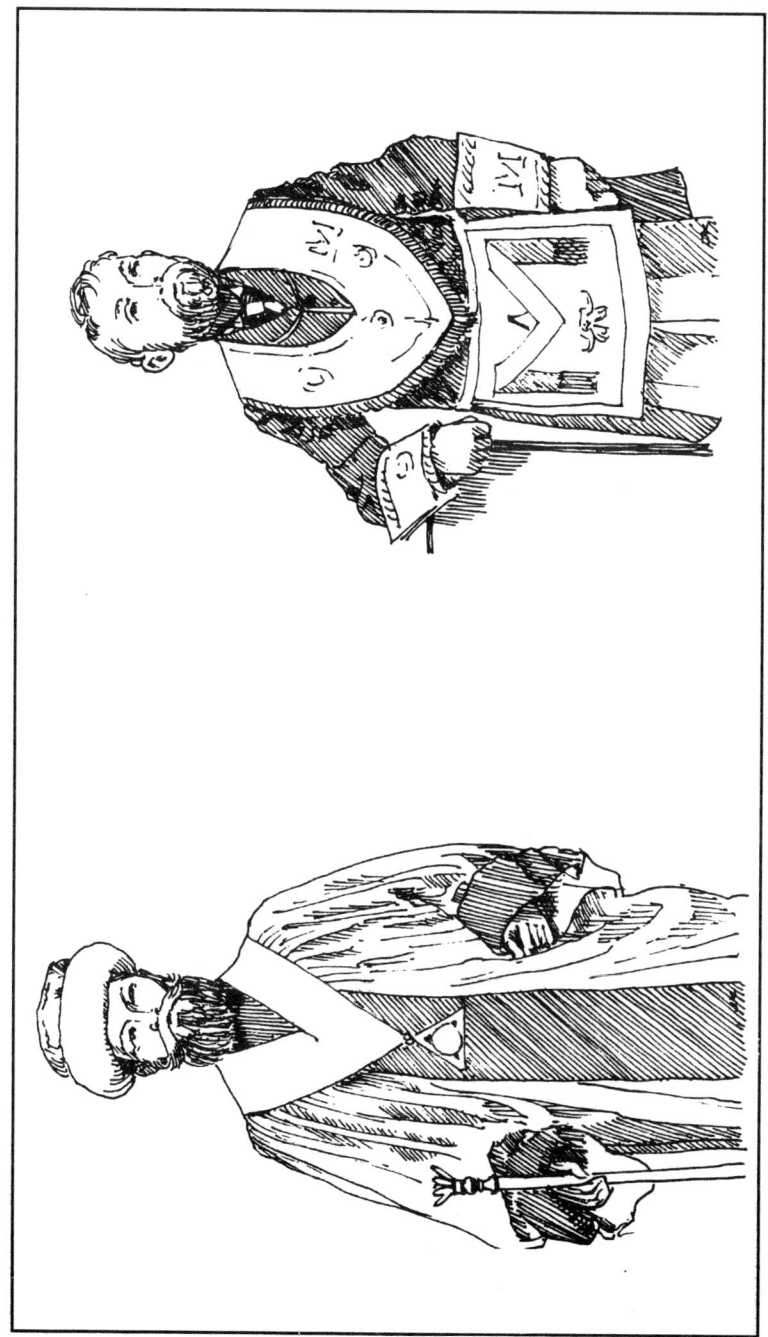

Plate VI

A Freemason *A non-Freemason*
(Royal Arch, nineteenth century) *(Royal Antediluvian Order of Buffaloes, nineteenth century)*

Plate VII – Friendly Society aprons using Masonic symbolism
top: Odd Fellows apron   bottom: apron of Friendly Society

CERTIFICATES

The practice of issuing certificates goes back to the eighteenth century, and these 'clearance certificates' were issued by Lodges to members who were about to leave the Lodge, usually because they were either moving away or wished to visit a Lodge in another area. When the holder settled somewhere else and wished to join a Lodge in his new locality, he would produce this certificate to show that he was a regular Freemason and had left his previous Lodge 'in good standing' that is, he had paid his annual dues up to the point at which the certificate was issued. When visiting other Lodges the certificate could be produced to verify his credentials. All the early certificates were handwritten documents and it was not until 1756 that they were issued in an engraved and printed form.

Lodge and Grand Lodge certificates

Since 1813, when The United Grand Lodge of Antient Free and Accepted Masons of England was formed, all those who attained the degree of Master Mason have been entitled to a Grand Lodge certificate and could not obtain any other Masonic certificate without one. These certificates give the name of the Mason, the name and number of the Lodge, the date of initiation and the date of registration with The United Grand Lodge as a Master Mason. The date is shown both as AL (anno lucis), the Jewish Year of Light, and AD (anno domini), the Christian Year of Our Lord.

Your ancestor's actual signature will be on the certificate, and by the signature may be written *'NE VARIETUR'*, which means that the signature must never vary in any way from the one shown. Pre-1813 certificates were issued only on request, but since this date have been issued to all Master Masons as a matter of course. Post-1813 certificates show the coat of arms of the Grand Master and are signed by the Grand Secretary as well as the recipient of the certificate. After 1813 and before 1963 these certificates were written both in English and Latin. On some travelling certificates there may be a physical description of the Freemason concerned, even in one case down to his Roman nose. (Plate VIII.)

Other certificates

Different certificates are issued for various orders and events other than Craft Masonry. Masons who contributed to charities such as the Royal Masonic

Plate VIII – A United Grand Lodge Certificate in English and Latin.

Institution for Girls, the Freemasons' Hospital and Nursing Home and the Royal Masonic Hospital, received certificates which give name, Lodge number and name, the part they played and the date. If you have one of these certificates the Grand Charity Trust or the Lodge shown may be able to assist you with further information. The museum at Freemasons' Hall has examples of all types of certificates, or you can make enquiries by post.

The United Grand Lodge states that a Grand Lodge certificate must not be framed and displayed at home or at work by the Freemason concerned.

ARTEFACTS

China

In 1756 or thereabouts a method of transfer printing on pottery was discovered which made possible the large scale manufacture of jugs, plates, etc. which found their way into private homes. Items including Goss china were decorated with Masonic devices or armorial bearings. Refreshment being an important part of the proceedings, china decorated with Masonic symbols was produced for use in Lodges, and many of these items were presented to members on Masonic occasions. These presentations may have been inscribed with the name of the Lodge or the member's name. There is a large collection on display in the museum at Freemasons' Hall in London which includes Masonic Meissen and Chinese export porcelain of the Chi/en Lung, 'famille rose' period, 1735-95.

Plate IX – Masonic artefacts
Locket (French prisoners' work)   *Tortoishell cased Masonic watch and two watch cocks*

Glass

Masonic 'firing glasses' are small glasses with Masonic decoration which have strengthened bases made to withstand rapping on the table to express appreciation when toasts were made. There is also glassware of every size and shape, decorated with Masonic emblems, especially a 'fruiting vine' pattern.

Plate

Items of gold and silver were made in the form of commemorative, presentation or association pieces, and many were inscribed with names or occasions. Snuff and cigarette boxes, pipes, watches, cufflinks and other personal accessories were also made in many types of metal. (Plate IX.)

Unless a specific Lodge is indicated where an enquiry could initially be made, you should contact or visit the museum at Freemasons' Hall where there is a comprehensive collection of all these items. There are many illustrations of this collection in *Freemasons' Hall* by J Stubbs and T O Haunch (1983).

MASONIC CHARITIES

The Grand Charity

The Grand Charity supports Masons and their dependants in need, and originates from the Committee of Charity, 1727, which was originally for brethren and their dependants when they were in distressed circumstances. The Grand Charity was formed in 1980 to allow greater emphasis on giving to non-Masonic charities than had previously been allowed by its predecessor, the Board of Benevolence.

There are five Royal Masonic Institutions which are of interest to family historians.

The Royal Masonic Institution for Girls

1788 Founded as The Royal Cumberland School for the Daughters of Indigent Freemasons at Somers Place East, Euston Road, London, and started with fifteen girls between five and ten years old.

1795 Moved to St George's Fields, now Westminster Bridge Road, London.

1853 Moved to St John's Hill, Wandsworth Common, London; renamed Royal Freemasons' School for female children and in 1868 renamed The Royal Masonic Institution for Girls.

1918 Junior school moved to Weybridge, Surrey and closed in 1973.

1934 Senior school moved to Rickmansworth Park, Rickmansworth, Hertfordshire WD3 4HF, from where it still operates.

The Royal Masonic Institution for Boys

1794 Royal Cumberland Freemasons' School. Freemasons' Hall has a list of candidates 1790-93 covering candidates' name and ages, with the name of a petitioner. A child could not be less than 5 or more than 9, had to be without infirmity and having had smallpox.

1798 Two Masonic charities were formed for clothing, educating and apprenticing the sons of indigent or deceased Freemasons. In 1808 a prospectus was issued with details of clothing to be worn and which subjects would be taught whilst the boys, aged 5 to 14, were living in their own parishes. Widows were to receive £10 a year for boys until the age of 5. In 1816 a list of names of candidates was issued and this included age, the Lodge number, occupation and address of the father, why help was needed and details of other members of the family. These two documents of 1808 and 1816 are on view in an exhibition at Freemasons' Hall.

1832   Renamed The Royal Masonic Institution for Boys.

1857   Lordship House, Wood Green, Tottenham, London, purchased and by 1863 there were 100 boys in residence.

1903   A new school was built in Bushey, Hertfordshire, where by 1939 there were 800 boys aged 8 to 18. The school closed in 1977.

In the library at Freemasons' Hall, London, there are volumes of the Royal Masonic Institution for Boys Annual Reports 1861-1954. They contain lists of patrons, officers, committees, governors, subscribers and boys. Details regarding the boys vary, and some include dates of admission, with ages and achievements, some also give father's name and Lodge number.

In May 1994 *Family Tree Magazine* reported that in the library of the Girls' School at Rickmansworth there is a memorial book of soldiers who were killed in the First World War, who had attended the Masonic Boys' School either as pupils or teachers. There are biographical details, service histories, and causes of death; sometimes the place of burial is stated, and for some there is a photograph. For The Old Boys' Association, contact Mr M Mullally, 16 Grandville Road, Limpsfield, Oxted, Surrey RH8 0DA.

The Masonic Trust for Boys and Girls

In the early 1980s the Royal Masonic Institution for Girls and the Royal Masonic Institution for Boys merged, by Act of Parliament, to become the Masonic Trust for Girls and Boys which is Registered Charity No. 285836, and they 'continue to relieve poverty and provide an education and preparation for life for the children of the family of a Freemason and, where funds permit, for any children, as their fathers would have done, had they been able to do so.' The Trust's Mission Statement, which includes a short history of the Charity, can be seen at 31 Great Queen Street, London WC2B 5AG.

The Royal Masonic Benevolent Institution

1836   The Asylum for aged and decayed Freemasons was announced, and by 1842 the Masonic Benevolent Annuity Fund was set up.

1850 A home at Croydon, Surrey, was built and was combined with the annuity scheme and formed the Masonic Benevolent Association.

1960 Residential facilities began to expand with the provision of sheltered accommodation and residential homes.

The Royal Masonic Hospital

1913 Freemasons purchased the Chelsea Hospital for Women in Fulham Road, London, and it then became the Freemasons' War Hospital and Nursing Home.

1933 Royal Masonic Hospital, Ravenscourt Park, London W6 was opened and all patients paid according to their means; if they were unable to do so they had access to the Samaritan Fund. It was closed in 1996, at which time a new Masonic Samaritan Fund was set up for Freemasons and their dependants if they are unable to obtain treatment.

Two of the institutions mentioned above have been closed, and three are in a transitional state. Their histories and the records of those involved are difficult to obtain or co-ordinate. For details of the amount of information available, contact Freemasons' Hall, London, or the Royal Masonic Benevolent Institution.

BASIC STARTING POINTS FOR RESEARCH

Your research may begin at one of four starting points:

Known – Lodge name or Lodge number

In the *Masonic Year Book* Lodges in existence are shown alphabetically and numerically together with the Province. Enquire at the Lodge, the Provincial Grand Lodge or the United Grand Lodge of England.

Known – name only

In the absence of a photograph, unfortunately there is no full chronological or alphabetical list of members except an alphabetical register up to 1814, held at the United Grand Lodge of England.

Known – photograph with approximate date

The United Grand Lodge of England may identify the Province or Lodge, and from the regalia the office held in either. This information could lead to research in the appropriate records.

Known – name, abode or place of work

If before 1967 begin by consulting Quarter Sessions records; the relevant Provincial Grand Lodge may also be able to help.

GENERAL COMMENT

What can you find out about your Masonic ancestors? This booklet is an introduction, and it may help you locate records which give a man's age upon joining a Lodge, his place of residence, his occupation, and, if the secretary of his Lodge has been diligent, the date of his death or details of transfer to or from another Lodge. This information is particularly valuable before civil registration in 1837, as it may point the way to a date of birth or death which has been difficult to ascertain. You may also be able to find family connections that have been elusive, as men were often in a Lodge with relatives and social companions who could have married into the family.

If Lodge records are missing from 1799 up to 1967, the Quarter Sessions records may provide information on the man's residence and occupation. A systematic search from year to year could be a useful guide to any change of residence and occupation both before civil registration and after, when it may be possible to find a date and place of movement between censuses. Background information can be useful, for example Military Lodges in regiments or the militia, prisoners of war and Masonic immigrants and emigrants.

I have mentioned the tiny forget-me-not worn under the lapel, and you may have inherited various other artefacts, which are now collectors' items, such as regalia, (aprons, jewels etc.) china, glass, watches and other items too numerous to mention. There are ways to identify these. It may be possible to find a photograph or illustration of an ancestor, male or female, whom you have never seen in person, and personal signatures can be found on many records.

In this 'time of openness' some are more open than others, and as in all research perseverence is needed. The response to queries in one Masonic Province may not be the same in another. Lodges appear to be autonomous with regard to their historical records. There is no co-ordinating policy so that methods, information available, and charges or donations vary over the whole country. When making any enquiries it is necessary to remember that most of those contacted are voluntary helpers, and because of this have limited time available to answer queries. Contacts I have made myself have been helpful, so do not hesitate to enquire. The amount of material available varies, much has been destroyed over the years or until now has lain uncatalogued and possibly in unsuitable storage places. Always provide full details and background information with your enquiry and indicate what you want to know and why. Remember always to include an s.a.e. To begin to understand this complicated subject, which up to now has been perceived as inaccessible information for family historians, it would be an advantage to read some or all of the books in the select bibliography, most of which can be borrowed through your county library.

To paraphrase W S Gilbert, it is possible not only to find 'corroborative detail to add artistic verisimilitude' to your family history, but you can add to your genealogical knowledge and illuminate your ancestors' position in the local and social history of their time.

SELECT BIBLIOGRAPHY

Hamill, J and R A Gilbert, *World Freemasonry* (London, 1991)

Jones, B, *Freemasons' guide and compendium,* 2nd. edn. (London, 1956)

MacMulty, W Kirk, *Freemasonry* (London, 1991)

Mendoza, H, *Serendipity* (London, 1995)

Stubbs, J and T O Haunch, *Freemasons' Hall* (London, 1983)

United Grand Lodge of England, *The Constitutions* (London, current edition)

United Grand Lodge of England, *Masonic Year Book* (London, current edition)

USEFUL ADDRESSES

Freemasons' Hall, Museum and Library, Great Queen Street, London WC2B 5AZ
Telephone 0171 831 9811

Grand Lodge of Ireland, Freemasons' Hall, 17 Molesworth Street, Dublin 2
Telephone 003531 676 1337

Grand Lodge of Scotland, Freemasons' Hall, 96 George Street, Edinburgh EH2 3DH
Telephone 0131 225 5304

Masonic Trust for Girls and Boys, 31 Great Queen Street, London WC2B 5AG
Telephone 0171 405-2644

Royal Masonic Benevolent Institution, 20 Great Queen Street, London WC2B 5BG
Telephone 0171 405 8341

United Grand Lodge of England, Freemasons' Hall, Great Queen Street, London WC2B 5AZ
Telephone 0171 831 6021

Provincial Grand Lodges of England and Wales

Any communications should be sent to the Provincial Grand Secretary.

Bedfordshire	Bedfordshire Masonic Centre, The Keep, Bedford Road, Kempston, Bedford, MK42 8KJ
Berkshire	Berkshire Masonic Centre, Mole Road, Sindlesham, Wokingham, Berkshire RG41 5DB
Bristol	Freemasons' Hall, 31 Park Street, Bristol, BS1 5NH
Buckinghamshire	Beaconsfield Masonic Centre, Windsor End, Beaconsfield, Buckinghamshire HP9 2JW
Cambridgeshire	2 Lewis Crescent, Great Abington, Cambridge, CB1 6AG
Cheshire	36 Clay Lane, Timperley, Altrincham, Cheshire WA15 7AB
Cornwall	St. Mary's House, Cyril Road, Truro, Cornwall TR1 3TA
Cumberland and Westmorland	Masonic Hall, Gordon Street, Workington, Cumbria CA14 2RT
Derbyshire	Derby Masonic Hall, The Grange, 457 Burton Road, Little Over Derby, DE23 6XX
Devonshire	Freemasons' Hall, 27b Gandy Street, Exeter, EX4 3LS
Dorset	46 Fernhill Avenue, Weymouth, Dorset DT4 7QY

Durham	8 The Esplanade, Sunderland SR2 7BH
Essex	2 Station Court, Station Approach, Wickford, Essex SS11 7AT
Gloucestershire	Masonic Hall, Venn's Acre, Wotton-under-Edge, Gloucestershire GL12 7BE
Guernsey and Alderney	La Collette, Les Croutes, St. Peter Port, Guersney, Channel Islands
Hampshire and Isle of Wight	85 Winchester Road, Chandler's Ford, Eastleigh, Hampshire SO53 2GG
Herefordshire	Bramleigh, The Square, Yarpole, Leominster, HR6 OBA
Hertfordshire	Fleet House, Royal Road, St. Albans, Hertfordshire AL1 4LQ
Isle of Man	Ballachrink Cottage, Ballakeirn, Port Soderick, Braddan, Isle of Man IM4 1AY
Jersey	35 Elizabeth Avenue, St. Brelade, Jersey, Channel Islands JE3 8GR
East Kent	Masonic Library and Museum, St. Peter's Place, Canterbury, Kent CT1 2DA
West Kent	Oakley House, Bromley Common, Bromley, Kent BR2 8HA
East Lancashire	Freemasons' Hall, Bridge Street, Manchester, M3 3BT
West Lancashire	Masonic Hall, 22 Hope Street, Liverpool, L1 9BY
Leicestershire and Rutland	Freemasons' Hall, 80 London Road, Leicester, LE2 ORA
Lincolnshire	Masonic Hall, Cambridge Road, Grimsby, Lincolnshire DN34 5SZ
Middlesex	122 Gunnersbury Lane, London W3 9BA
Monmouthshire	46 Pettingale Road, Croesyceiliog, Cwmbran, Gwent NP44 2PH
Norfolk	Provincial Office, 47 St Giles Street, Norwich, Norfolk NR2 1JR
Northamptonshire and Huntingdonshire	Freemasons' Hall, St George's Avenue, Northampton, NN2 6JA
Northumberland	Neville Hall, Westgate Road, Newcastle-upon-Tyne, NE1 1SY
Nottinghamshire	Masonic Hall, Goldsmith Street, Nottingham, NG1 5LB
Oxfordshire	31 The Leys, Chipping Norton, Oxfordshire OX7 5HJ
Shropshire	'Roseberry', 21 Stanham Drive, Ellesmere, Shropshire SY12 ONU
Somerset	The Masonic Hall, Church Street, Wedmore, Somerset BS28 4AB

Staffordshire	211 Tettenhall Road, Wolverhampton, WV6 0DD
Suffolk	Freemasons' Hall, Soane Street, Ipswich, Suffolk IP4 2BG
Surrey	71 Oakfield Road, Croydon, Surrey CR0 2UX
Sussex	Sussex Masonic Centre, 25 Queen's Road, Brighton, Sussex BN1 3XA
North Wales	8 Mostyn Avenue, Craig-y-don, Llandudno, Gwynedd LL30 1YS
South Wales Eastern Division	7 Guildford Street, Cardiff, CF1 4HL
South Wales Western Division	Iet yr Eithin, Llanwnda, Goodwick, Pembrokeshire SA64 0HX
Warwickshire	2 Stirling Road, Edgbaston, Birmingham, B16 9SB
Wiltshire	33 Wrde Hill, Highworth, Swindon, Wiltshire SN6 7BX
Worcestershire	94 Birmingham Road, Bromsgrove, Worcestershire B61 0DF
Yorkshire, North and East Ridings	Freemasons' Hall, Duncombe Place, York, YO1 2DX
Yorkshire, West Riding	Masonic Hall, Spring Bank Place, Bradford, BD8 7BX

District Grand Lodges abroad

Many Lodges were formed from the eighteenth century onwards and addresses can be found in the Masonic Year Book.

INDEX

addresses, officers and secretaries'	5
Annual certificates	7
apron	23, 24
Master Mason's	10, 23
Ars Quatuor Coronatorum	12
Atholl Grand Lodge of 1753	2
brief history	2
certificates	8, 29, 30, 31
Channel Islands	17
charities	29, 34
china	32
Commonwealth Grand Lodges	5, 13
constitutions and regulations	4
Constitutions, The	2, 3, 4, 5, 11
county record offices	8, 20
Craft Lodge	1, 5, 8, 11, 24
officers	3
Criminal Law Act	8
Data Protection Act	6
District Grand Lodges	5
District Grand Lodges abroad	43
English Speculative Masons	23
First World War memorial	4
Foreign Grand Lodges	5, 13
forget-me-not	1, 38
Freemasons' Hall	2, 4
library	12, 19
museum	1, 20, 24, 33
Freemasons' magazines	20
French prisoners' work	32
Friendly Societies	20, 22, 26, 28
genealogical information	4
glass	33
Grand Charity	34
Grand Lodge of Ireland	16, 41
Grand Lodge of Scotland	16, 41
Grand Master	2, 4
Grand Officer	3
Grand Rank, 1717 to 1968	5
Grand Temple	4
handbook	13
Honourable Fraternity of Ancient Freemasons	14
Internet	21
jewels	11, 17, 24, 25
Grand Lodge Officers'	9
Letchworth's bookshop	4
Lodge membership books	7
Lodge records	11
Lodge secretaries	13
London Grand Rank Officers	3
Masonic	
funerals	19
halls	11, 13
officers	3
orders	5
regalia	17, 24
Masonic Peace Memorial	4
Masonic Trust for Boys and Girls	35
Masonic Year Book	4, 5, 11, 12
Masons' Company	14
Masons' Guilds	2
Master Mason	11, 24
Master of a Lodge	2
membership books	4, 11
Military Lodges	12, 16
monumental inscriptions	19
Nazis	1
newspapers	19-21

openness	2, 11, 38
Operative Masonry	2, 23
Order of Women Freemasons	14
Other certificates	29
other orders	12
plate	33
Premier Grand Lodge of 1717	2
prisoners of war	17
Private Lodges	8
Provincial Grand Lodge	8
Provincial Grand Lodges	5, 41
handbooks	11, 12
officers	3
Provincial Lodge	13, 24
Quarter Sessions records	7, 8, 11, 12, 16
for garrison towns	16
Quatuor Coronati Lodge No. 2076	12
regalia	23, 26
registered number	11
requirements	2
roll of honour	18
Royal Antediluvian Order of Buffaloes	19, 22, 26, 27
Royal Masonic Benevolent Institution	35
Royal Masonic Hospital	36
Royal Masonic Institution for Boys	34
Royal Masonic Institution for Girls	34
Royal Society	2
Second World War	18
secret society	7
Seditious Societies Act, 1799	16
signature	16, 29
Speculative Masonry	2
square and compasses	22
Trade Guilds	23
trade unions	20, 22, 26
transactions	12
travelling certificates	29
Travelling Lodges	16

travelling warrants	16
United Grand Lodge	1, 2, 16, 41
library	5
rule book	5
United Grand Lodge of Antient, Free and Accepted Masons of England	2, 3
Wales	3
war memorials	18
women Freemasons	14
World War One peace memorial	18
Worshipful Master	3, 10, 11, 24
Year Book	4, 5, 11, 12